SCIENCE

CRACKERS

Bubbling
BIOLOGY

Steve Parker

QED Publishing

Created for QED Publishing by Tall Tree Ltd
Editors: Rob Colson and Jennifer Sanderson
Designers: Jonathan Vipond and Malcolm Parchment
Illustrations, activities: Lauren Taylor
Illustrations, cartoons: Bill Greenhead

Copyright © QED Publishing 2011

First published in the UK in 2011 by
QED Publishing
A Quarto Group company
226 City Road
London EC1V 2TT

www.qed-publishing.co.uk

A catalogue record for this book is available from the British Library.

ISBN 978 1 84835 564 4

Printed in China

Picture credits
(t=top, b=bottom, l=left, r=right, c=centre, fc=front cover)
Dreamstime: 5tl Surpasspro, 6r, Smileus, 13c Stephankerkhofs, 23c Jubalharshaw19; **Getty
Images:** 4l Michael Kappeler, 20t Gary Vestal, 21br Frederic Pacorel; 22–23 Visuals
Unlimited, Inc./Andy Murch; **iStockphoto** 27b rotofrank; **Science Photo Library:** 4tr Eye
of Science; 5b Ron Austing, 7b Adrian Bicker, 23t Power and Syred; **Shutterstock** 3 and 7t
clearviewstock, 3cr and 14 Betacam-SP, 3br photazz, 5cr Khoroshunova Olga, ,6b maigi,
7c Lim Yong Hian, 8l kesipun, 8–9 Lowe Llaguno, 9tr Quest786, 9br Bogdan Wankowicz,
12l Vishnevskiy Vasily, 12r Mircea Bezergheanu, 13tl orionmystery@flickr, 13tr Jiri Vavricka,
13br hagit berkovich, 16b mariait, 16t Anyka, 17t Gentoo Multimedia Ltd, 17c Roman
& Olexandra, 17br Rufous, 18 br Pelana, 20b and 31 ravi, 21l Sebastian Kaulitzki, 22r
paulaphoto, 25b F.C.G., 26c Stefan Fierros, 26b Trevor Kelly, 27t Dave Green, 27cl Wolfgang
Staib, 27cr SunnyS, 28t Steve Bower, 28bl Becky Sheridan, 28bl Trykster, 28br Kolaczan, 29t
Stephen Dalton, 29b Image Focus

Note
Website information is correct at time of going to press. However, the publishers
cannot accept liability for any information or links found on any Internet sites,
including third-party websites.

In preparation of this book, all due care has
been exercised with regard to the activities
and advice depicted. The publishers regret
that they can accept no liability for any loss
or injury sustained.

The practical activities in this book have been
checked for health and safety by CLEAPSS, an
organization that provides practical support
and advice on health and safety in science
and technology.

Words in **bold** are explained
in the Glossary on page 31.

CONTENTS

BIO-WORLD!

Living things are found on almost every part of our planet, from the bottom of the sea to the highest mountain. They can survive in nearly any conditions.

Living things range from germs that are too tiny to see, and bugs smaller than the dot on this 'i', to huge blue whales and giant redwood trees. Some animals and plants are very common, while others live only in one specific place. Biology is the study of life, and it groups living things depending on what they do.

TINIEST BUGS

A magnifier or microscope makes small things look bigger and shows us a fascinating world of tiny creatures. This is the face of a minibeast called a tardigrade. About 20 of them would fit in this letter 'o'.

FASTEST MOVERS

Nearly all animals move in some way. The fastest land animal is the cheetah. It races along at 110 kilometres per hour – almost three times faster than a sprinter.

FASTEST HUMAN 43 KM/H

SUPER TREES

Trees grow fast and tall in bright, warm sunshine. They are home to many animals who eat their leaves, flowers and fruits, make nests in their branches, and dig tunnels among their roots underground.

IMAGINE THIS...

We can help animals, plants and nature in many ways. One simple way is not to leave litter, which can injure wild animals and cause pollution.

BAMBOO FEAST

Many animals and plants are very rare and threatened by climate change and human activity. There are fewer than 3000 giant pandas in just a few places in China. These creatures eat almost nothing but bamboo.

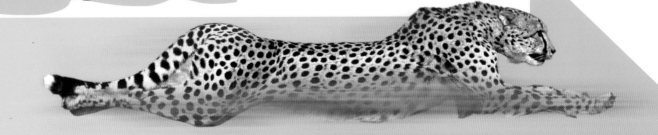

CHEETAH 110 KM/H

GREEN AND GROWING

Seaweeds on the shore, soft mosses on a riverbank, tall conifer trees, beautiful flowers, rustling grass, bushes with delicious fruit, trees without leaves in winter – all these are plants.

Plants grow using sunlight. Their green leaves soak up sunlight and use the energy to make food such as sugars. To do this, they take in carbon dioxide, a gas from air, and give out another gas called oxygen. Most plants have leaves held up on a stem or stalk. Many plants lose their leaves and stop growing in winter. They start again when it is bright and warm in spring. Trees have thick, strong stems called trunks, made of wood. At the bottom are roots. These hold the plant in the soil, and take up water and mineral substances for it to grow.

EVERGREENS
Plants that keep their leaves all year round are called evergreens. Conifers, such as pines, and firs, make their seeds in woody cones.

SEAWEEDS
Seaweeds are a type of algae. They do not have proper roots because they have water and nutrients all around them. But many have root-like parts called holdfasts that stick them to the rocks.

6

SUNSHINE

Most plants grow best with bright sunshine, warmth and plenty of water in the soil. The trunks of trees hold their leaves up high, away from the shade and nearer the Sun.

IMAGINE THIS...

Some plants need a lot of sunshine to grow strong. Others have adapted to grow in places where there is little sunshine, such as a forest floor beneath thick trees.

FRONDS

Ferns have large, divided leaves, called fronds. They spread by sending out stems that grow along the ground and then sprout new fern plants.

MOSSES

Mosses are small, low plants with soft, spongy leaves. They do not have flowers. Mosses prefer cool, damp, shady places like the banks of rivers and streams and among rocks.

FANCY FLOWERS, SUPER SEEDS

Plants do not grow flowers so that we can admire their beautiful colours and lovely scents. Flowers are a plant's way of reproducing, or making more of its kind.

Most flowers have male and female parts. The male parts make tiny pollen grains. These must get to the female parts of flowers. This is known as **pollination**. Some pollen grains are blown by the wind, while others are carried by animals. When plants are pollinated, they can start making their seeds. When seeds find the right conditions, usually damp soil, they start to grow or **germinate** into young plants.

IMAGINE THIS...

Some plants and flowers look pretty but they can be harmful. They might cause a skin rash or sneezing. Before touching unfamiliar plants, check with someone who knows if they are safe or not.

Pollen basket

POLLEN CARRIER

Bees are common carriers of pollen grains. The grains stick to the bee's body and legs. Some bees also have special pollen baskets to carry the pollen. The bee also takes some pollen back to its home as food.

FLOWERING TIME

Most plants grow their flowers during the warm seasons of spring and summer. In deserts, flowers come out after rain, before the land dries out again.

BRIGHT AND SCENTED

A flower's bright petals, its smell, or scent, and its sweet liquid, called nectar, all attract animals such as this hummingbird. As the bird feeds on nectar, pollen grains stick to its feathers. The bird then carries the pollen to other flowers.

NEW SHOOTS

When seeds land in the right conditions, they start to germinate. They make shoots, which grow leaves. Roots grow down into the soil, hold the plant in place and take up water and nutrients.

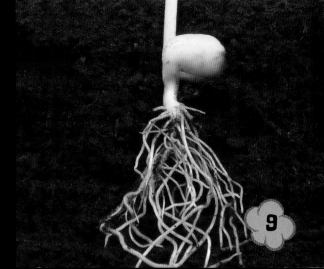

GET GROWING

See how water can start a small seed growing into a whole plant, using food stored inside the seed.

YOU WILL NEED:

- large bowl
- water
- dried bean seeds
- tall clear jar
- kitchen towel
- large sponges

1 Fill the bowl with water and add the beans. Leave overnight.

2 Press sheets of kitchen towel against the jar sides. Add the sponges to the jar so that they press the kitchen towel against the sides of the jar.

3 Poke several seeds about halfway down inside the jar between its sides and the paper, so you can see the seeds from the outside.

4 Pour about 2 cm of water into the bottom of the jar. Make sure it soaks into the paper so that the seeds are damp.

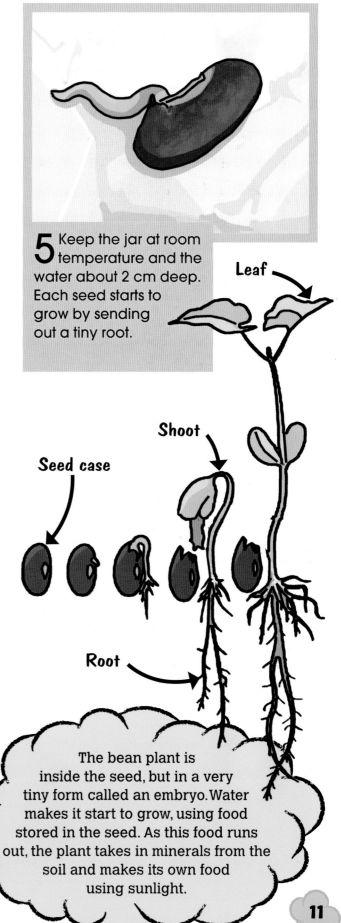

5 Keep the jar at room temperature and the water about 2 cm deep. Each seed starts to grow by sending out a tiny root.

Leaf

Shoot

Seed case

Root

The bean plant is inside the seed, but in a very tiny form called an embryo. Water makes it start to grow, using food stored in the seed. As this food runs out, the plant takes in minerals from the soil and makes its own food using sunlight.

6 Gradually the root gets longer. Then a green shoot grows out of the seed case. After a few days, the seed will run out of food, so ask an adult to plant it in a pot of soil. Keep watering and watch it grow!

LOOK AND LISTEN

Animals need to know what is around them, including food or enemies. They do this with their senses, such as seeing and hearing.

All kinds of animals have eyes to detect light. Animals that are out at night have extra-large eyes to detect as much light as possible. Ears are used to pick up sounds. The important hearing parts of the ears are inside the head. Birds have ears under their feathers. Reptiles, such as snakes, have ears that are thin patches of skin just behind the eye.

Snake ear

BIG-EYED HUNTER

Owls have large eyes to see their victims from far away, even in the dark. Light goes into the eye through the dark-looking hole, called the **pupil**. After light enters the pupil, it hits the lens. The lens focuses light to make a clear picture.

IMAGINE THIS...
Eyes are important but also very delicate. Make sure you protect yours, for example by wearing sunglasses in bright sunlight.

INSECT EYES

The eyes of insects are like hundreds of tubes joined together. Each part sees just a tiny area, but all these areas join together for the whole wide view.

HEARING IN WATER

Fish have a stripe along each side of the body called the **lateral line**. This senses sounds, such as the clicks of a dolphin, and also ripples and movements nearby, like the swish of a shark.

EXTRA-BIG EARS

The fennec fox's huge ears catch the tiniest sounds – even beetles or ants crawling across the ground. This is how the fox finds its food.

OPTICAL ILLUSIONS

Think you can trust what you see? Think again! Sometimes patterns and shapes can be arranged to fool your eyes and brain into seeing something that isn't actually there. This is called an optical illusion.

1 Hold the page upright and stare at the centre of the spiral spokes. Slowly twist it left and right. Do the spokes twist?

2 Can you see grey spots flashing in the white circles? Now try to focus on just one of the spots. Does it disappear?

14

3 Your eyes can trick the way you see shapes! Look at the spaces between where the lines meet. Can you see circles?

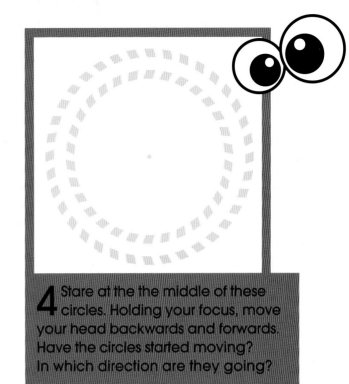

4 Stare at the the middle of these circles. Holding your focus, move your head backwards and forwards. Have the circles started moving? In which direction are they going?

5 What do you see first when you look at this picture – a man playing the saxophone or the face of a woman? Can you see the other shape?

6 This illusion is all about lines. The red square looks like its sides are bending in. But its sides are actually straight.

ON THE MOVE

All animals move around during their lives. Even creatures that seem to be stuck down, such as shellfish and sponges on the seashore, moved around before they settled on the rocks.

Birds and bats fly, fish and dolphins swim, and moles and earthworms burrow in soil. On land, some creatures walk and run, while others hop, jump or slime along. Snakes have no legs, but they can slither quickly. In fish, reptiles, birds and mammals, muscles pull the bones of the skeleton inside, to move the legs and other body parts. In creatures such as insects, spiders and crabs, the muscles are inside the body casing and pull on the casing to move the legs, claws and other parts.

FLYING

Most insects, such as this cockchafer, have wings and flap them to fly. The wings move down and back to push the insect up and forwards. Some flies flap their wings more than 500 times each second!

RUNNING

Long legs are the sign of a fast runner, like this horse. The legs can cover lots of distance with each stride or step, pulled by muscles in the shoulders and hips.

SOARING

Some birds gain height without flapping by turning into the wind. This is known as soaring. A seabird, such as this albatross, can soar without flapping for days!

SWIMMING

Fish, such as eels, swim by bending their bodies from side to side. The body, fins and tail push against the water and move the fish forwards.

IMAGINE THIS...

Wild animals use their muscles to keep them fit. Humans are the same. Stay active, exercise and keep your muscles healthy!

FIXED DOWN

Shellfish, such as these barnacles, begin their lives as small young called larvae. They swim, float and drift in the water until they find somewhere suitable to live. Then they stick down and stay there.

REFLEXES

Sometimes you make a sudden movement that you cannot control. This is called a reflex. It is an automatic action that you do not have to think about, usually to protect your body from harm.

YOU WILL NEED:

- torch
- mirror
- dim room

2 Shine a torch on your face, but NOT straight into your eye. Watch the pupil. It should rapidly get smaller. After a minute, switch off the torch and watch. The pupil should gradually get bigger again.

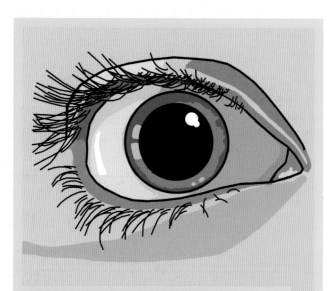

1 Spend a few minutes in a dim room, then look in the mirror. Note the size of your pupil (the black hole in the middle of your eye).

The coloured ring around the pupil is called the **iris**. In bright conditions it makes the pupil smaller to prevent too much light damaging the eye. In dim conditions it opens wider to let in more light.

REACTIONS

How fast are your reactions? And do they get faster with practice? A reaction is when you make a deliberate quick movement or action after something happens.

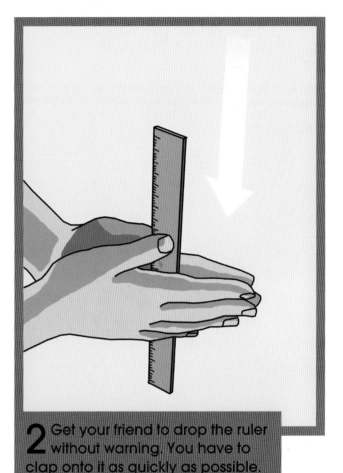

2 Get your friend to drop the ruler without warning. You have to clap onto it as quickly as possible. The measurement where your thumb is shows your score.

1 Ask your friend to dangle the ruler with the zero-end down. Put your hands close together with your thumbs on either side of the ruler, level with the bottom of it, as if ready to clap.

Do this several times. As your reactions get faster, your thumbs should be farther down the ruler, and the measurement will be smaller. Is your friend faster or slower than you?

BITE AND SWALLOW

Some animals only eat plants, and they are called **herbivores**. Others eat mostly meat, and they are **carnivores**. Animals that eat both plants and animals are called **omnivores**.

The biggest land animals, such as elephants, rhinos and hippos, are all herbivores. They have wide teeth for chewing grasses, leaves and twigs. There are also much smaller herbivores. Mice gnaw seeds with their long, sharp front teeth.

Different carnivores hunt in different ways. Big cats creep near their prey, then rush at it. Eagles swoop down from the sky and grab victims with their sharp talons. Other carnivores are small but deadly because they have venom.

TOOTHY!

Big cats like this lion have very long, sharp teeth called canines near the front of the mouth. These stab into victims to kill them and then rip them to pieces for swallowing.

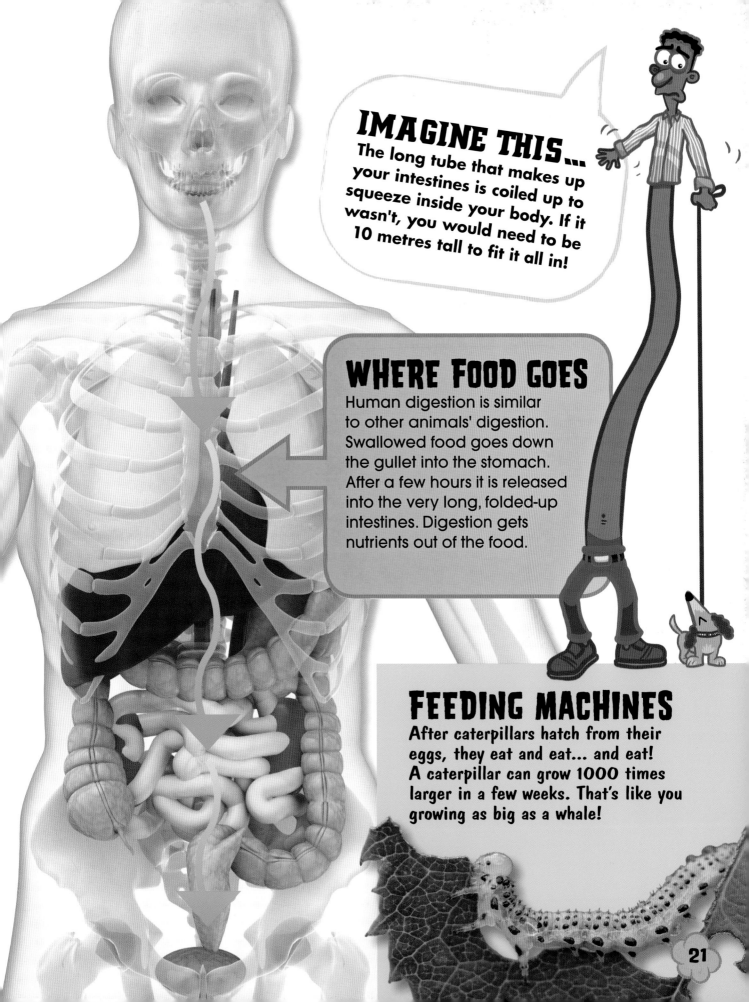

IMAGINE THIS...

The long tube that makes up your intestines is coiled up to squeeze inside your body. If it wasn't, you would need to be 10 metres tall to fit it all in!

WHERE FOOD GOES

Human digestion is similar to other animals' digestion. Swallowed food goes down the gullet into the stomach. After a few hours it is released into the very long, folded-up intestines. Digestion gets nutrients out of the food.

FEEDING MACHINES

After caterpillars hatch from their eggs, they eat and eat... and eat! A caterpillar can grow 1000 times larger in a few weeks. That's like you growing as big as a whale!

PANT AND PUMP

All animals need a gas called oxygen, which is in the air around us. They get it by breathing. Then the blood, pumped by the heart, spreads the oxygen and also nutrients around the body.

Mammals, birds and reptiles breathe with two sponge-like parts in the chest, called **lungs**. These suck in fresh air, take in the oxygen, and blow out the stale air. There is oxygen in water too, where creatures breathe using parts called **gills**. A fish's gills are on the sides of its head, under flaps of skin. The heart is a strong pump, like a bag made of muscle. As it beats, it pushes blood around the body. All body parts need supplies of blood to bring them oxygen and high-energy nutrients, and to take away any waste.

BREATHING AND SOUNDS

Air coming out of the lungs can be used to make sounds by shaking, or vibrating, a part in the neck called the voicebox (larynx). This is how people sing, dogs bark and tigers roar.

BIG GILLS

Fish breathe as water flows in through the mouth, over the curved gills, and out through slits on the sides of the head. The gill slits on a basking shark are bigger than you!

INSIDE BLOOD

Blood contains millions of tiny parts called cells. Rounded red cells carry all-important oxygen. Pale white cells attack any germs that get into the body.

SEEING BLOOD

In some small creatures, such as this daphnia, you can see the blood and count the heartbeats. The hearts of little animals beat hundreds of times every minute. A blue whale's heart beats about 10 times a minute.

IMAGINE THIS...

Most creatures have one heart. But an octopus has three, and a worm has five! However, a worm's hearts are like thick tubes, rather than proper pumps.

23

FITNESS FUN

When your body gets busy, running or playing sport, your breathing and heart speed up. This sends more blood, with oxygen and nutrients, to your muscles. Count your heartbeats using your **pulse**. This is the throb of a blood vessel in your wrist that is caused by the surge of blood made by each heartbeat.

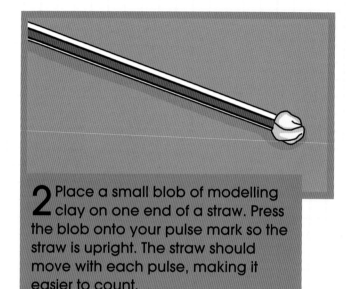

2 Place a small blob of modelling clay on one end of a straw. Press the blob onto your pulse mark so the straw is upright. The straw should move with each pulse, making it easier to count.

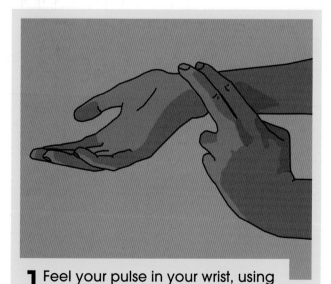

1 Feel your pulse in your wrist, using two fingers from the other hand. Put a small mark with the pen where it feels the strongest.

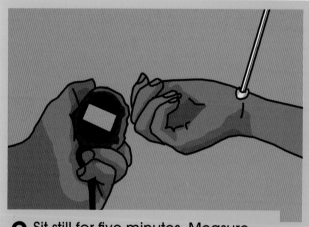

3 Sit still for five minutes. Measure and record your pulse over 15 seconds, then do the same with your breathing. Multiply these numbers by four to give your pulse and breathing rates per minute.

4 Take off the straw and jog on the spot for two minutes. This will make you breathe more rapidly. Sit down and put the straw back quickly. Measure your pulse and breathing as before. Repeat until both slow down to the resting rate again.

Draw a graph of the results, like those shown here. See how your breathing and heart speed up when you are active, then slowly return to their resting rates.

Pulse rate (Beats per minute)

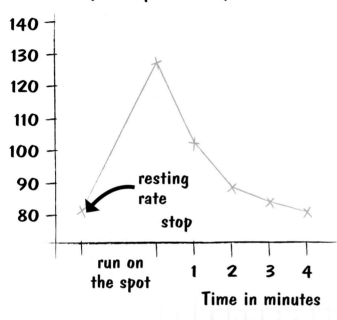

resting rate

stop

run on the spot

1 2 3 4

Time in minutes

Breathing rate (Breaths per minute)

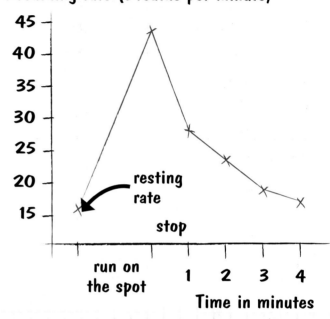

resting rate

stop

run on the spot

1 2 3 4

Time in minutes

GETTING FIT

Top athletes exercise every day to get fit. This means that they can exercise for longer and will recover quickly after physical activity.

MAKING MORE ANIMALS

All living things make more of their kind – it is one of the main features of life. It is known as breeding, or **reproduction**. But different creatures do it in many ways.

Most animals lay eggs, usually in a place that is safe for the young when they hatch. Butterflies lay eggs on leaves so that the caterpillars are already on their food. Some creatures look after their eggs and also the babies. Birds keep their eggs warm, and feed and protect the baby chicks. Mammals like whales and humans have babies rather than laying eggs. The mother mammal feeds her babies on her milk.

CHANGING SHAPE

Some creatures change shape a lot as they grow up. This is known as **metamorphosis**. A frog's eggs hatch into tadpoles with tails. Then the tadpole's legs appear, its tail shrinks and it becomes a young frog.

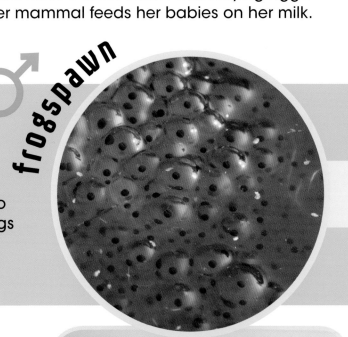

frogspawn

HATCHING

Baby crocodiles hatch from eggs, which have been kept warm in the soil or a pile of rotting plants. As soon as they emerge, they start to hunt small animals such as grubs and flies.

FAST GROWING

A young seal pup feeds on its mother's milk for about two weeks after it is born. The milk is rich in nutrients, so the pup grows fast. It is soon able to swim and feed on fish instead.

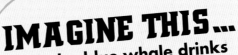

IMAGINE THIS...

A baby blue whale drinks 225 litres of its mother's milk every single day! A human baby drinks only about 1 litre each day.

MILK

tadpole

frog

CARING FOR YOUNG

Bird parents spend so much time feeding their youngsters, they hardly have time for themselves. This blue tit will make over 200 feeding trips every day for its squawking chicks.

LOOK OUT, DANGER!

Wild places can be dangerous. Many animals and plants have special tricks and skills to defend themselves against enemies and stay alive.

Some creatures, such as snails, crabs and shellfish, have hard shells to protect them. Prickly spines are a good defence, as in hedgehogs, sea urchins and also plants such as the cactus. Another trick is to look like your surroundings so that enemies do not notice you. A young deer has a spotted coat to help it hide in the undergrowth. This is known as camouflage. Some places have harsh seasons, such as an icy-cold winter. One answer is to go into a long sleep, called hibernation. Another answer is to move away on a long journey, or migration.

ARMOUR
The armadillo has hard plates over its body to guard against **predators**, such as coyotes and cougars. It can dig fast and partly hide in a hole with just its hard back showing.

SPINES
A cactus does not have wide, flat leaves. Instead its leaves are long, sharp spines. These keep away plant-eating animals who want to munch on its juicy stem.

DEEP SLEEP

As winter approaches, the dormouse feeds hungrily and puts on weight as stores of body fat. These keep it going through its long winter sleep, in a nest among leaves and roots.

IMAGINE THIS...

The record for the longest migration is held by the Arctic tern. Every year it flies 40,000 kilometres between the far north and far south.

MIGRATION

When the dry season begins, plant-eaters like wildebeest and zebra start their migration. They walk hundreds of kilometres to places where rain has fallen and fresh plants have grown.

NOW YOU SEE ME...

See how camouflage works by making a really wild scene to test on your friends.

YOU WILL NEED:

- card
- coloured pens
- scissors

1 Draw a nature scene on a large piece of card with dark brown trees, bright red flowers, vivid green grass and blue sky.

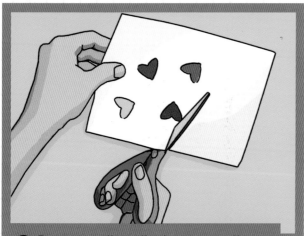

2 Draw small moth shapes on the card and colour them in brown, red, blue and green. Cut them out.

3 Put them on the scene so one of each four is camouflaged on its own colour and the others are on the other colours.

See how many moths your friend can spot in three seconds. If your friend was a hungry bird, he or she would notice the moths that were not camouflaged, and eat them first.

GLOSSARY

CARNIVORE
An animal that eats other animals.

GERMINATE
When a plant seed starts to grow.

GILLS
The parts of a fish that sit behind its head. They take oxygen out of the water so that the fish can breathe.

HERBIVORE
An animal that eats plants.

IRIS
The coloured part of the eye, which sits around the pupil.

LARYNX
Also known as the voicebox. This is the part of the neck where your voice comes from.

LATERAL LINE
The sensitive line that runs along the side of a fish. It detects sounds and movements underwater.

LUNGS
Sponge-like body parts in the chest of many animals. They allow oxygen to pass into the body and carbon dioxide to pass out of it.

METAMORPHOSIS
When an animal changes greatly in shape as it grows from a baby into an adult.

OMNIVORE
An animal that eats both plants and other animals.

POLLINATION
When the male and female parts of a plant join together to create seeds.

PREDATOR
An animal that hunts other animals.

PULSE
The regular beating made by your blood as your heart pushes it through your blood vessels.

PUPIL
The black hole in the centre of the eye, which allows light into the eyeball.

REPRODUCTION
When plants and animals make more of their own kind.

INDEX

FURTHER INFORMATION

www.bbc.co.uk/schools/ks2bitesize/science
Click on living things to find out all about plants and animals.

www.kidsbiology.com/biology_basics/index.php
This website is packed with information and biology facts.